Bridge is for Kids

Bridge with Patty!

Introduction

Bridge is a great game. It has all the things you like in a game. Strategy, competition, puzzles, rewards and best of all....IT'S FUN.

You can just play bridge for fun with your friends or if you really like it and are willing to study you can become a really good player and play in state, national and international tournaments.

In these first few classes you'll get a chance to just see what the game is all about, how much you like it and decide how good you want to get.

For now just enjoy learning a new game and good luck!

How Bridge is played.

Bridge is played by four people playing with a regular deck of playing cards which holds 52 cards (we don't use the jokers in bridge). It's a partnership game and the person sitting across the table from you is your partner; the two people to your right and left are your opponents. Many times you'll see a plastic mat on the table with a number and the words North-South-East-West.

This is called a **'table mat'.**

- **North and South are partners**

- **East and West are partners.**

In every deck of cards there are four suits.

- **Clubs ♣,**
- **Diamonds ♦,**
- **Hearts ♥, and**
- **Spades ♠.**

Since there are 52 cards in the deck and there are 4 suits...

$$52/4 = 13$$

There are 13 cards in each suit.

The highest/strongest card in each suit is the Ace...the lowest/weakest is the two. The order of strength within each suit is

Ace..King..Queen..Jack..Ten..9..8..7..6..5..4..3..2

Strongest		Weakest

The highest five cards in each suit are called "honor cards".

The Honor Cards are the

Ace – King – Queen –Jack – Ten

Sometimes in this book and other books about bridge you'll see the honor cards listed by the first letter of their name. **A – K – Q – J -T**

There are three parts to the game:

- Bidding, telling your partner in a special code we have just for bridge about the number of cards you have in each suit and how many of the strong cards you have.
- Playing, physically playing each of the cards in your hand.
- Scoring, awarding points for one of the partnerships.

The first thing we do is 'Deal' the cards.

To start the game the cards are shuffled (mixed up) and handed out to the four people at the table. The player dealing (handing out) the cards starts with the player sitting to his left and deals the cards one at a time to each player (going clockwise) until the cards are gone.

Since there are 52 cards in the deck and we have four players....

$$52/4 = 13$$

**Each person playing will have 13 cards.
Those 13 cards are called a 'hand'.**

You should count your cards every time they are dealt to make sure that you have thirteen.

Sort

Once you have your thirteen cards you will put all of the clubs together, all of the diamonds together, all of the hearts together and all of the spades together. Usually players put red cards, then black, then red then black. You don't have to but players usually arrange the cards highest to lowest within each suit. This action is called 'sorting your hand'. After you are finished your hand would look something like this:

The next thing after dealing and sorting your cards would be bidding. Bidding is the toughest thing to learn and takes the most time, so we're going to save that for later and instead do something fun...Play.

Play

Bidding decides who gets to play the first card, but since we're saving bidding for last....we'll just decide one person will play the first card. Let's say North gets to play the first card.

The player who plays the first card is called the 'Opening Leader'.

Playing our 13 cards each time is called a 'Hand of Bridge'.

Bridge with Patty!

Bridge players use the word 'hand' to mean the thirteen cards they are holding and also to mean playing those thirteen cards.

After the first card is played, the person to the left of the opening leader would play a card, then the third person and then the fourth person.

Those four cards, one played by each player, are called a 'Trick'.

Since every player has thirteen cards, there are thirteen tricks in every hand of bridge.

Playing your thirteen cards

There are two types of hands you might play in bridge. The first type is a hand of bridge in which *the only cards that can win are the highest card played in the suit that was led*. That kind of hand is called a **No Trump** hand.

The second type of hand is called a hand with a Trump Suit. We'll discuss that in a little while.

The rules for No Trump play are:

- Opening leader can play (lead) any card they choose,
- If a player has a card in the suit that was led, they must play that suit,
- If a player does not have a card in the suit that was led, they can play (called a 'discarding' or 'throwing away') any card they choose,
- The highest card **in the suit that was led** wins the trick,
- **Whoever wins the trick, leads first to the next trick** and they may play any card they choose.

What you will discover is that, in a No Trump hand, the types of things that help you win tricks for your side is honor cards...Aces, Kings, Queens and Jacks. But you will also find that long suits can help you win tricks.

Remember that to win a trick a player must play the highest card *in the suit that was led*. When you have a long suit you may find that you are on lead and that no player has any cards left in your long suit. If you play the ♦2 and you are the only person that has any diamonds, your ♦2 will win the trick!

Let's see what that might look like. North is the opening leader and is playing the first card. East will play the second card, South will play the third card and West will play the last card.

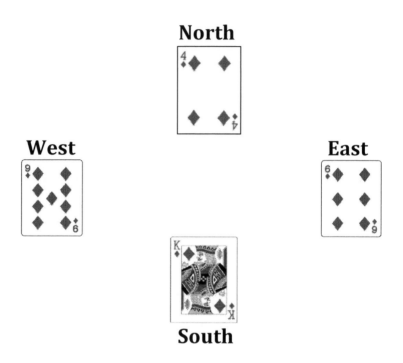

North

West   **East**

South

- South played the highest card, in the suit was led, so North/South win the trick.
- South played the card that won the trick for his partnership.
- South would lead the first card to the next trick

The four cards played at that first trick would be turned face down, in front of the person who played the card and the long portion of the card would be placed in the winning partnerships direction. It would look like this.

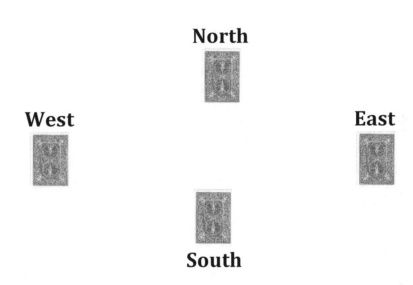

North

West   **East**

South

As subsequent tricks are played the cards will be turned face down in the same manner. All the cards in every player's hand will be played, one at a time, until all their cards are gone.

When all thirteen cards have been played the table would look like this. In this hand North/South won 10 tricks and East/West won 3 tricks.

North

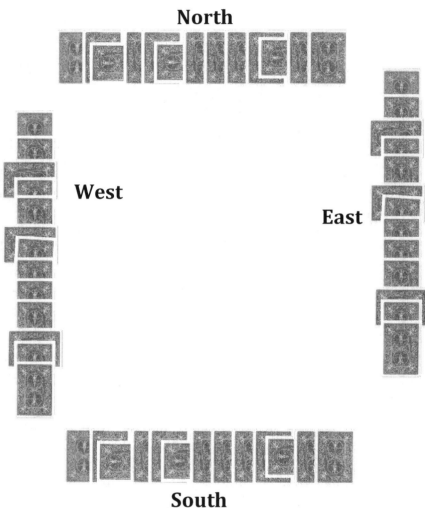

West

East

South

Each player would count the number of tricks their partnership had won. After everyone agrees how many tricks each side took, a score (awarding points to one of the partnerships) would be assigned to the hand. (At this point you don't how the score is decided. Be patient, we're getting there!) The cards would then be mixed together, the deck shuffled and the cards would be dealt to begin the next hand.

The winner of an entire game of bridge is decided after determining the score for a number of different hands.

When you played this hand, you might have noticed that you won tricks by playing high cards and you probably won some tricks with low cards if no one else at the table had any cards left in the suit you led.

In No Trump hands players usually win tricks with:

- **Honor cards (As, Ks, Qs, Js and 10s), and**
- **Small cards in long suits.**

Trump Suit Play

Sometimes in the bidding a suit will be declared 'trumps'. You don't know how that works yet, since we haven't talked about how the bidding works, but be patient...we're getting there!

When there is a trump suit (clubs, diamonds, hearts or spades), there is another method for you to win a trick. A trick can be won by playing a card in the suit that was declared trumps. The smallest trump is bigger/stronger than a card in any other suit. An example: If hearts were declared trumps and my opponent led the ♠A and I had no spades in my hand, I could play the ♥2 and win that trick.

The rules for playing when there is a trump suit are:

- Opening leader can play (lead) any card they choose,
- If a player has a card in the suit that was led, they must play that suit,
- If a player does not have a card in the suit that was led, they can choose to play a trump or they can discard any card they choose,
- The highest card in the suit that was led wins the trick *unless a trump was played*,

- If a trump was played, *the highest trump played wins the trick*,
- Whoever wins the trick, leads first to the following trick and they may play any card they choose.

In the example below hearts are trumps. North is on lead and has led the ♦4.

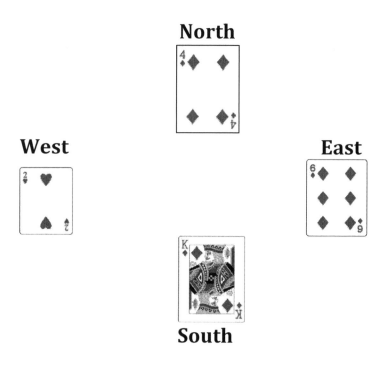

North

West

East

South

West does not hold any diamonds. Hearts are trumps. West will 'trump' South's ♦K. West's ♥2 will win this trick since the lowest trump is stronger than the highest card in any other suit.

What you will find is that if your partnership has at least eight cards in one suit between their two hands (this is called a 'fit'), that taking tricks becomes much easier. If you have more than eight....you'll probably take a lot more tricks that you expect.

In a Suit (trump) contract you usually take tricks with:

1) Honor cards (As, Ks, Qs, Js and 10s), and
2) Maybe the small cards in a long suit (but this isn't as likely) and by
3) Trumping.

How the rest of the game is played

In the bidding, one side will say that they expect they can take a certain number of tricks in the play. They are called the 'Declaring' side.

The opposing partnership are called the 'Defenders' and they will be trying to keep the Declaring side from taking the number of tricks which they said they would take....the number for which they have 'contracted'.

When the declaring side is set in the bidding, one partner will be the *'Declarer'* and their partner the *'Dummy'*.

Declarer is player who bid the suit that is trumps (or No Trump) the first time in the bidding.

The opponent to the left of Declarer is the *'Opening Leader'* and plays the first card.

Dummy, after the opening lead, will put their hand face-up on the table in rows with trumps on the right.

Declarer will tell Dummy what card is played at each trick.

Everyone will play all of their cards and will count how many tricks each side won.

One partnership will get points (we're going to talk about how many points in the scoring chapter coming up next).

Then the next hand is dealt and we do everything again.

Quiz - The Basics

1) How many cards are there in a deck of cards? _____

2) What are the four suits? _____   _____

   _____   _____

3) How many tricks are there in every hand you play?
   _____

4) What is the highest card in the deck?_____

5) Who wins the trick in a No Trump hand?

   _____

EXTRA CREDIT

Explain trumps.

_____

_____

_____

Scoring

Only one partnership scores in each hand of bridge. As you probably noticed, it is much easier to take tricks if a partnership has more high cards and/or more trumps than their opponents, so the people who invented bridge decided to give the declaring side a handicap...like in golf.

The declaring side (the partnership who gets to name trumps) must win six tricks **before** they get to count tricks towards the number they said (declared) they would take in the bidding.

These first six tricks are called 'Book'. If the partnership which, in the bidding, declared that they would take a certain number of tricks, takes that many tricks, they will get points. Their points will come from two sources:

- Trick Score
- Bonuses

Trick Score

A trick score is awarded based on which suit was declared trumps. In bridge two of the suits are called *major* suits (Hearts and Spades) and the other two suits are called *minor* suits (Diamonds and Clubs). If the trump suit was:

- Spades or hearts 30 points are awarded for each trick after book (the first six tricks won by the declaring side).
- Diamonds or clubs, 20 points are awarded for each trick after book (the first six tricks won by the declaring side).

If the partnership declared that no suit would be trumps, a No Trump hand, then:

- 40 points are awarded for the first trick after book (the first six tricks won by the declaring side) and then 30 points for each subsequent trick.

If the declaring side does not win the number of tricks they declared they would win, they receive no points. Instead the defending side will win points.

TRICK SCORE

No Trump
40 points for the first trick
30 points for every other trick

Spades and Hearts
30 points for each trick

Diamonds and Clubs
20 points for each trick

*Graphic
sponsored by* ♥ Atlanta
♠ Junior
♣ Bridge

Bridge with Patty!

Bonuses

A small bonus (called a '**part-score**' bonus) of 50 points is awarded to a partnership which wins the number of tricks they declared they would win. However, the declaring side can be awarded larger bonus points if the declaring side thinks that:

- They have strong hands and/or good trumps, and
- They are willing to risk declaring they can win a large number of tricks, and
- They win the large number of tricks they declared they would win.

The large bonuses which could be awarded are:

- **Game**, for declaring that your side will win ten tricks with hearts or spades as trumps, eleven tricks with diamonds or clubs as trumps or nine tricks with no trump suit.
- **Slam**, for declaring that your side will win twelve tricks.
- **Grand Slam**, for declaring that your side will win thirteen tricks

GAME SCORE
(300 or 500 point bonus)

4 Hearts or **4 Spades**
25/26 HCP

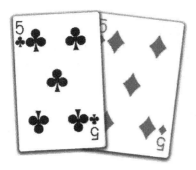

5 Clubs or 5 Diamonds
28/29 HCP

3 No Trump
25/26 HCP

*Graphic
sponsored by*  **Atlanta
Junior
Bridge**

Bridge with Patty!

Defender Scoring

When a declaring side does not win the number of tricks which they declared they would win (this is called 'going down' or 'getting set' or 'not making their contract'), then the defenders are awarded points. The defenders will win a certain number of points for every trick the declaring side goes down. They win either 50 or 100 points for each trick.

We'll talk later about how you know whether you win 50 or 100 for each trick.

Quiz - Scoring

1) Which are the major suits? _____ _____

2) Which are the minor suits? _____ - _____

3) How many points do you get for every trick in a minor suit? _____

4) If you bid 4♣, how many tricks would you need to win to make your contract ? _____

5) What is book?

_____

EXTRA CREDIT

If your contract is 3♠ and you win ten tricks, how many points would you earn?

Bidding

Bidding is a conversation between you and your partner to discuss:

- The strength of your hand, how many Aces, Kings, Queens and Jacks you hold, and
- The number of cards you have in each of the suits, the **distribution** of your hand.

Every bid you make is going to tell partner something new about your hand. Something you think they'd like to know.

You're talking about the strength of your hand so you and partner can decide if you want to try and get one of those big bonuses.

You're talking about the number of cards you have in each of the suits so you and partner can decide if, between your two hands, you have enough cards in a suit to want that suit to be named trumps.

In the 1910's a man named McCampbell came up with an idea to make it easier to talk about the strength of your hand. He said that you could add a certain number of points for each high card you held.

POINTS

 Ace = 4 points

 King = 3 points

 Queen = 2 points

 Jack = 1 point

Graphic sponsored by Atlanta Junior Bridge

Bridge with Patty!

Adding all of those points together and remembering that we have four suits,

$$(4+3+2+1) = 10$$

$$10 \times 4 = 40$$

There are 40 High Card Points (HCP) in a deck of cards.

It has been mathematically determined that if, between your and partner's hand, you hold 25 or 26 HCPs your partnership should have enough high cards to try to win the game bonus if you can play No Trump or if Spades or Hearts are trumps.

If you want to play with either Clubs or Diamonds as trumps, your side would need 28 or 29 HCPs between your and partners hand to try to win the game bonus. Why that difference?...because you and partner would have to bid to 5♦ or 5♣ for game in a minor suit. To take more tricks you usually need more strength and/or more trumps!

Remember from the chapter on scoring that, if a major suit is trumps you are awarded more trick points than if a minor suit is trumps. You should remember from playing hands that it was much easier to take tricks if you had a trump suit than with just high card. So, if given a choice between a major suit as trumps or no trump, pick a major suit.

Your priority in choice of contracts should be:
1. Majors
2. No Trump
3. Minors

This thought is the reason for all the beginning rules you will learn about bidding a hand.

You will be talking about your *distribution* to find out if you have a at least eight cards in a suit between your two hands (called a *'fit'*) in a major suit that you can name/declare trumps.

You will be talking about your *strength* to determine if you and partner have enough HCPs to attempt to bid high enough to win a bonus.

If you do not have a fit in a major suit, think of No Trump before you think about playing with a minor suit as trumps. All these ideas are based on how the scoring works.

We're trying to make decisions that give our side the best score on each hand that we think is possible.

Every once in a while you will reach a point in the bidding when partner is trying to get you to tell them more about your hand and you've already told them everything you think is important. At that point your message will be "Enough already! I don't have anything else to tell you that you don't already know."

Bidding, with all the rules you have to learn, is really hard. Most people like playing the cards much better.

Remember that bidding helps you to make sure that you and partner play with the best/longest suit as trumps between your two hands and helps you decide about trying for those big bonuses.

Bidding is really important so that you and partner can make sure you get the best score possible on every hand you play!

Opening the Bidding

The cards are dealt, each player counts their cards (make sure you have 13!), sorts their hand, and counts their HCPs. The player who dealt the cards has the first chance to talk to his partner about his hand.

If dealer does not have 12 HCPs in his hand he will say the word 'Pass'. Pass says "I do not have at least 12 HCPs".

If dealer has 12 HCPs he will make a bid other than Pass. His bid will be a number and a suit (or No Trump). That bid will be in a code we are learning which will begin to describe our strength and distribution to our partner. The first player to bid something other than 'Pass' becomes the *'Opening Bidder'*.

If dealer passes (says the word Pass), then dealer's left hand opponent (LHO) has an opportunity to talk to his partner. If LHO bids something other than pass, LHO has become the Opening Bidder. If LHO passes, then the third person at the table has an opportunity to talk.

The bidding is over when there is a bid other than pass and the next three people pass or if there are four passes.

Never think that you have to tell the story of your hand with just one bid and no other bids being made. Remember that the bidding is a conversation. It may be a short conversation or a longer conversation, but is almost never a single bid followed by three passes. Opening Bidder and his partner (who is called '**Responder**') may talk back and forth several times and tell each other several pieces of information before they decide how high they want to bid and which suit they would like to be trumps (or to play No Trump.

Remember

Every bid you make should tell partner something they don't know about either your strength or distribution.

Opening Bids of One of a Suit

If you have at least 12 points you will do something other than 'Pass'. Your choice of an opening bid will be in this order of what you look for first to tell partner:

- With five cards or more in hearts or spades you will open 1♥ or 1♠
- With two five card suits you will open the highest in rank
- Without a five card or longer major you will open a minor suit
- With one longer minor you will open your minor (with exception below in last two bullet items)
- With two three card minors you will open 1♣ (you can remember this as a club has three petals)
- With two four card minors you will open 1♦ (you can remember this as a diamond has four points)
- With five or more diamonds and four clubs you will open 1♦
- With five clubs and four diamonds and 12-16 points you will open 1♦

- With five clubs and four diamonds and 17+ points you will open 1♣

When you first learn bridge you probably won't understand why these rules are set up in this order and why you have to follow them. Most people have trouble remembering all of the rules. However, these rules were created to make that conversation that you and partner are having more clear and easier when you and partner get to your second and third bids...your '**rebids**'.

WHAT SHOULD I OPEN?

MAJOR SUIT

1♥ OR 1♠ ..... 12–21 POINTS;
5 CARDS OR LONGER

NO TRUMP

1 NT................ 15–17 POINTS; NO VOID,
NO SINGLETON
NO FIVE CARD MAJOR

2NT................ 20–21 POINTS; NO VOID,
NO SINGLETON
NO FIVE CARD MAJOR

3 NT................ 24–26 POINTS; NO VOID,
NO SINGLETON
NO FIVE CARD MAJOR

MINOR SUIT

1♣ OR 1♦ ..... 12–21 POINTS; 3 CARDS
OR LONGER AND
NO FIVE CARD MAJOR

IF YOUR MINOR SUITS ARE
EQUAL IN LENGTH:
5/5 OPEN 1♦
4/4 OPEN 1♦
3/3 OPEN 1♣

Graphic sponsored by  **Atlanta Junior Bridge**

Bridge with Patty!

Quiz - Bidding

1) How many points can you count for each of the honor cards?
Ace _____ King____Queen_____Jack_____Ten_____

2) Which player has the first chance to open the bidding? _____

3) How many points do you need to open the bidding?_____

4) What is the first thing you look for when you are deciding what to open? _____

5) How many cards do you need in a minor suit to open the bidding 1♣ or 1♦?

_____

EXTRA CREDIT

If you do not have five cards or more in a major suit and you hold three clubs and three diamonds, which suit would you open? _____

Responding to an Opening Bid of One of a Suit

After a player opens the bidding their partner becomes 'Responder'. Responder has a different set of rules. Responder will bid if they have 6 points. The priority of what bid is chosen in responding changes dependent on whether partner opened one in a major suit or one in a minor suit.

Partner has Opened 1♣:

- 6+ points and a five card major bid your major. If you have five hearts and five spades; bid 1♠
- 6+ points and a four card major bid your major. If you have four hearts and four spades; bid 1♥
- 6-10 points and a balanced hand with no 4 card or longer major bid 1NT
- 11-12 points and a balanced hand with no 4 card or longer major bid 2NT
- 13-15 points and a balanced hand with no 4 card or longer major bid 3NT
- 6-9 points and five or more clubs (a 'fit') bid 2♣
- 10-12 points and five or more clubs (a 'fit') bid 3♣
- 6+ points and four or more diamonds with an unbalanced hand bid 1♦

Partner has Opened 1♦:

- 6+ points and a five card major bid your major. If you have five hearts and five spades; bid 1♠
- 6+ points and a four card major bid your major. If you have four hearts and four spades; bid 1♥
- 6-9 points no 4 card or longer major and no diamond fit bid 1NT
- 6-10 points and a balanced hand with no 4 card or longer major bid 1NT
- 11-12 points and a balanced hand with no 4 card or longer major bid 2NT
- 13-15 points and a balanced hand with no 4 card or longer major bid 3NT
- 6-9 points and five or more diamonds (a 'fit') bid 2♦
- 10-12 points and five or more diamonds (a 'fit') bid 3♦
- 10+ points and four or more clubs and an unbalanced hand bid 2♣

Partner Opens 1♣ or 1♦
Your Response:

0-5 pts Pass

6-9 pts weak

Bid 1 of a MAJOR: ♠ or ♥ with 4+ cards in the major suit

Bid 1 No Trump (6 – 10)

Raise your partner's Suit to the 2-level with 5 or more trumps

10-12 pts Invitational

Bid 1 of a MAJOR: ♠ or ♥ with 4+ cards in the major suit

Jump to 2 No Trump (11-12 pts) with a balanced hand

Bid a New Suit

Raise your partners suit to the 3-level with 5 or more trumps

13+ pts game

Bid 1 of a MAJOR: ♠ or ♥ with 4+ cards in the major Suit

Jump to 3 No Trump with a balanced hand

Bid a New Suit

Graphic sponsored by  Atlanta Junior Bridge

Partner has Opened 1♥:

With 3+ cards in partner's major (a 'fit'):

- 6-9 points raise partner's major to 2♥
- 10-12 points raise partner's major to 3♥
- 13+ points bid a new suit and raise partner's major to Game at your next bid
- Less than 7 points, five or more cards in partner's major and a singleton or void in another suit (this is called a 'Weak Freak') raise partner's major to 4♥

Without a fit for partner's major:

- 6+ points and four or more spades bid 1♠
- 6-9 points bid 1NT
- 10 points and a balanced hand bid 1NT
- 10+ points and an unbalanced hand or a good five-card (sometimes four-card) or longer suit bid your suit at the two level
- 11-12 points and a balanced hand bid 2NT
- 13-15 points and a balanced hand bid 3NT
- 16+ points and a balanced hand bid a new suit

Partner has Opened 1♠:

With 3+ cards in partner's major (a 'fit'):

- 6-9 points raise partner's major to 2♠
- 10-12 points raise partner's major to 3♠
- 13+ points bid a new suit and raise partner's major to Game at your next bid
- Less than 7 points, five or more cards in partner's major and a singleton or void in another suit (this is called a 'Weak Freak') raise partner's major to 4♠

Without a fit for partner's major:

- 6-9 points bid 1NT
- 10 points and a balanced hand bid 1NT
- 10+ points and five or more hearts bid 2♥
- 10+ points and an unbalanced hand or a good five-card (sometimes four-card suit) or longer suit bid your suit at the two level
- 11-12 points and a balanced hand bid 2NT
- 13-15 points and a balanced hand bid 3NT
- 16+ points and a balanced hand bid a new suit

Partner Opens 1♠ or 1♥
Your Response:

0-5 pts Pass

**6-9 pts
weak**

Raise your partner's Suit to the 2-level with 3 or more trumps

Bid a new suit at the One level

Bid 1 No Trump (6-10 pts)

**10-12 pts
Invitational**

Raise your partner's Suit to the 3-level with 3 or more trumps

Bid a new suit

Jump to 2 No Trump with a balanced hand (11-12 pts)

**13+ pts
game**

Bid a New Suit at the two-level (if hearts you must have 5+ to bid at two-level)

Jump to 3 No Trump with a balanced hand and no four card major that you can bid at the one level

Graphic sponsored by  **Atlanta Junior Bridge**

Responding to the Opening Bid

1) When your partner opens the bidding, what person do you become?_____

2) How many points do you need to respond to the opening bidder? _____

3) When your partner opens a minor suit and you have enough points to respond, what is the first thing you look for in your hand?_____

4) After partner has opened 1♣, how many cards do you need in hearts in order to bid 1♥? _____

5) After partner has opened 1♠, how many high card points (HCPs) and how many cards do you need in hearts in order to bid 2♥?

    # of Hearts needed _____ HCPs needed_____

EXTRA CREDIT

In the bidding, what is ranking of the four suits and No Trump?

_____   _____   _____   _____   _____

Lowest   Highest

Practice Hands for Suit Opening Bids

Board 1
North Deals
None Vul

♠ A 8 5 3
♥ Q 9 6 4 2
♦ A
♣ K 9 3

♠ J 9 7
♥ K 10 3
♦ Q J 9 4
♣ A 8 7

N
W E
S

♠ 10 4
♥ J 7 5
♦ K 10 7 6 5
♣ J 6 2

♠ K Q 6 2
♥ A 8
♦ 8 3 2
♣ Q 10 5 4

West	North	East	South
	1 ♥	Pass	1 ♠
Pass	2 ♠	Pass	3 ♠
Pass	4 ♠	Pass	Pass
Pass			

Opening Lead: Q♦, top of touching honors

1♥ = 12+ Points and 5+ hearts

1♠ = 4+ spades and 6+ points

2♠ = 12-15 pts and 4 spades

3♠ = an invitational hand. South is asking partner 'do you have 12 or 15?'

4♠ = I have enough since I have 13 pts and a singleton.

Practice Hands for Suit Opening Bids

Board 2
East Deals
N-S Vul

```
              ♠ A J 10 5
              ♥ A 10 9 5
              ♦ K 9
              ♣ Q 10 3

   ♠ 6 4 3          N           ♠ Q 9
   ♥ K Q 6      W       E       ♥ 7 4 3
   ♦ 8 7 2          S           ♦ A 6 5 4 3
   ♣ A 5 4 2                    ♣ J 8 6

              ♠ K 8 7 2
              ♥ J 8 2
              ♦ Q J 10
              ♣ K 9 7
```

West	North	East	South
		Pass	Pass
Pass	1 ♣	Pass	1 ♠
Pass	2 ♠	Pass	Pass
Pass			

Opening Lead: K♥, top of touching honors

1♣ = 12+ points and 3+ clubs

1♠ = 4+ spades and 6+ points

2♠ = 4 spades and 12-15 points

South passes since they do not have enough for game, since North would have bid 3♠ with a good 15 points. *Remember that 15 is the pivot point between 'minimum' and 'medium' hands.*

Practice Hands for Suit Opening Bids

Board 3
South Deals
E-W Vul

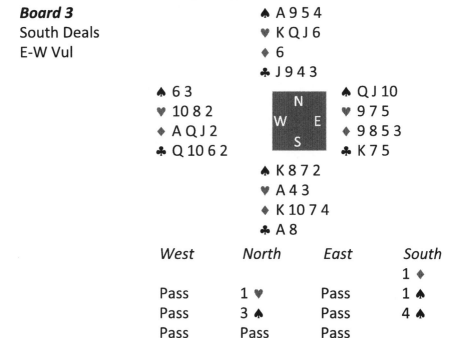

♠ A 9 5 4
♥ K Q J 6
♦ 6
♣ J 9 4 3

♠ 6 3
♥ 10 8 2
♦ A Q J 2
♣ Q 10 6 2

♠ Q J 10
♥ 9 7 5
♦ 9 8 5 3
♣ K 7 5

♠ K 8 7 2
♥ A 4 3
♦ K 10 7 4
♣ A 8

West	North	East	South
			1 ♦
Pass	1 ♥	Pass	1 ♠
Pass	3 ♠	Pass	4 ♠
Pass	Pass	Pass	

Opening Lead: 2♣, fourth from your longest and strongest *(Note: West would not lead a diamond because he would not underlead the ♦A.)*

1♦ = 12+ points and 3+ diamonds.

1♥ = 6+ points and 4+ hearts *(Remember: if you have two four card majors, bid hearts.)*

1♠ = I don't have four hearts, I have four spades.

3♠ = I also have four spades and I have 10-12 points.

4♠ = We have enough (25-26 pts) between our two hands to try for the game bonus.

Practice Hands for Suit Opening Bids
Board 4
West Deals
Both Vul

	North		
	♠ A K 10 2		
	♥ 10 4		
	♦ A 9 5		
	♣ 9 6 5 3		

West
♠ 8 6
♥ K Q 9 7
♦ K 4 3 2
♣ Q 8 4

East
♠ Q 9 7 4
♥ 8 6 2
♦ J 10 8 6
♣ A 10

South
♠ J 5 3
♥ A J 5 3
♦ Q 7
♣ K J 7 2

West	North	East	South
Pass	Pass	Pass	1 ♣
Pass	1 ♠	Pass	1 N
Pass	2 N	Pass	Pass
Pass			

Opening Lead: K♥, top of touching honors

1♣ = 12+ points and 3+ clubs

1♠ = 6+ points and 4+ spades

1N = 12-14 points, less than four spades, balanced hand
(Note: partner would have bid hearts before spades if he had four hearts. The only time he would have four hearts is if he had five spades. If so North will bid hearts at his rebid.)

2N = I have 11-12 points and a balanced hand

Pass = I have only 12 points. We do not have enough to try for game (25-26 pts).

Opener's Rebid

The important things Opener should ask himself at his second turn to call (his 'rebid') are:

- Do we have a major fit?
- Is it possible that we might have a major fit?
- If not, is it possible for us to play NT?
- Do I know if responder and I have enough points for game?
- Has responder limited the number of points he might hold?

The answer to those questions will help you choose your rebid. In general, if you know that you and responder do not have enough HCPs between your two hands to try for the game bonus, you should attempt to stay low and find a safe place to play.

Some basic rules for Opener's rebid are:

- A new suit at the lowest level limits opener's hand to 12-17 points and promises at least four cards in the suit he chooses to bid
- With 17+ points Opener can 'Reverse'
- With 18+ points Opener can bid a 'Jump Shift'
- With 18-19 points Opener can bid 2NT if they have a balanced hand

- If Opener raises responder's suit he will limit his hand to a 3-4 point range depending on the level to which he raises
- If Opener rebids 1NT he will show a balanced hand and limit his hand to 12-14 points
- If Opener rebids his own suit he will show at least six cards if bidding a major and at least five cards if bidding a minor suit; the level at which he bids describes the strength of his hand within 3-4 points

HOW STRONG IS MY HAND?

	OPENER	RESPONDER
MINIMUM	12-14/15 pts	6-9/10 pts
MEDIUM	15-17/18 pts	10-12 pts
MAXIMUM	18+ pts	13+ pts

Graphic sponsored by  Atlanta Junior Bridge

Responder's Rebid

The important things Responder should ask himself at his second turn to call (his 'rebid') are:

- Do we have a major fit?
- Is it possible that we might have a major fit?
- If not, is it possible for us to play NT?
- Do I know if opener and I have enough points for game?
- Has opener limited the number of points he might hold?

The answer to those questions will help you choose your rebid. In general, if you know that you and opener do not have enough HCPs between your two hands to try for the game bonus, you should attempt to stay low and find a safe place to play.

Some basic rules for Responder's rebid are:

- A new suit at the lowest level does not limit responder's hand and forces Opener to bid one more time
- If Responder returns to Opener's original suit at the lowest level he limits his hand to less than enough points for game and is simply saying 'of your two suits, we have more cards in this suit'

- If Responder rebids 1NT he will show a balanced hand and limit his hand to 6-10 points; a 2NT rebid will show 11-12 points; a 3NT rebid will show 13-15 points
- If Responder rebids his own suit at the lowest level he will show at least five cards and limit his hand to 6-9 points
- If Responder rebids his own suit skipping a level he will show at least six cards and limit his hand to 10-12 points

Counting for Distribution

After you and partner have discovered that you have a fit (eight cards in a suit between your two hands) you can add additional points to your hand for distributional features. Distributional features are singletons, voids and doubletons in suits other than your trumps suit that might be of benefit to your side when trying to win tricks.

Traditionally you are allowed to count:

- 3 extra points for a void,
- 2 extra points for a singleton, and
- 1 extra point for a doubleton.

Fair warning, a doubleton is not as valuable a feature and you should be cautious when adding points for that feature.

When speaking of adding these additional points, they are most commonly referred to as 'in support of <whichever suit you have bid and raised>". Meaning that because our partnership has bid and raised a suit, I now feel that these features will improve our chances of success in attempting game.

New ideas allow you add points for length, allowing you add one point for every card above four in a suit. Other new ideas allow you to count more points for distributional features that will be in dummy. There is not much difference between any of these methods...just don't add for length and shortness in the same hand. No Double Dipping!

Where do you Fall?

Opener

12   15/16   18/19   21
| Minimum | Medium | Maximum |

Responder

6   9/10   12/13   21
| Minimum | Medium | Maximum |

Quiz - Opener and Responder Rebids

1) Every time you bid what are you describing about your hand?_____ and

_____

2) When you open 1♣ and responder bids 1♥, how many hearts do you need to raise responder's heart suit?

_____

3) When opener raises responder's heart suit to 3♥, how many points does opener promise?_____

4) When responder raises opener's 1♠ opening bid to 2♠ and opener holds 19 HCPs, what should opener's bid as his second bid? _____

5) After opener has opened 1♠ and responder has bid 1NT, how many points and how many spades would opener promise if he bid 3♠?

# of Spades needed _____ HCPs needed_____

EXTRA CREDIT

If you had the hand below and opened 1♣ and your partner bid 1♠, what would you bid as your second bid?

♠Q2 ♥A72 ♦A65 ♣AKJ93

Opening the Bidding in Notrump

A Notrump (NT) opening bid promises a balanced hand (no singletons or voids) with no five-card or longer major. The level at which you open describes your HCPs (see chart on following page). Distributions considered a balanced hand are:

- 4-4-3-2,
- 4-3-3-3, and
- 5-3-3-2.

You may also open NT holding a semi-balanced hand (5-4-2-2), if that is the bid that allows you to best describe your hand. Consider opening NT with a semi-balanced hand when you have:

- 15-16 HCPs and your four card suit is a major suit, or
- When you have five clubs and four diamonds with only 15-16 points, and
- When your points are scattered amongst all of your suits, rather than concentrated in your long suits.

Opening NT follows these rules.

Point Range	Bid
15-17 HCPs	1NT
18-19 HCPs	Open a suit and rebid 2NT after a one-level response from partner.
20-21 HCPs	2NT
22-24 HCPs	Open 2♣ and rebid 2NT after partner's response.
25-27 HCPs	3NT

Responding to an Opening 1NT Bid

Responder's bids after partner has opened 1NT are very clear:

- With a four-card major suit and at least 8 HCPs, Responder will bid Stayman (see below).
- With a five-card or longer major suit, a five-card or longer major suit and at least 8 HCPs, Responder will bid Stayman.
- With a five-card or longer major and any number of points, Responder will bid a Jacoby Transfer (see below).
- With no four-card or longer major suit, Responder's bids are very easy. Simply do the math and decide if it is possible for you and opener to have enough points to attempt to win the game bonus.
  - With 0-7 HCPs Responder will pass.
  - With 8-9 HCPs Responder will bid 2NT; inviting opener to bid 3NT (game) with 16-17 HCPs.
  - With 10+ HCPs Responder will bid 3NT; as responder will know that their partnership has at least 25 HCPs between their two hands.

If Opener's opening NT bid was at the two-level, Responder's options are the same, however the point count necessary for his bids should be adjusted to compensate for the greater strength shown by Opener's 2NT opening bid.

Partner Opens
1 No Trump

Stop
0-7 Points

Invite
8-9 Points

GO
10+ Points

*Graphic
sponsored by*  **Atlanta
Junior
Bridge**

Bridge with Patty!

Jacoby Transfers

Jacoby Transfers, developed by Oswald Jacoby, have made several desired bidding sequences possible:

- To create a situation in which the no trump bidder would be declarer, which means that the opening lead would be coming into the strong hand and that the strong hand would be concealed;
- To enable responder, when he has a good two-suited hand, to show both of his suits; and

A Jacoby Transfer is:

- Used by responder to show a five-card or longer major;
- An instruction, a "relay" telling partner to bid the suit directly above the suit responder bid;
- An artificial bid. Responder is not showing or denying any holding in the suit that he has bid;
- An unlimited bid. Responder may have 0-25 points. He simply requires partner to bid the major suit he has shown; and
- Once agreed upon, always played. Jacoby Transfers, a 2♦ bid or a 2♥ bid will no longer be

a natural bid by responder after an opened or overcalled NT bid.

Note:
If you have 8+ HCPs, a five-card or longer major and a four-card major, bid Stayman - not Jacoby.

Hand 1		**Hand 2**	
North	South	North	South
1NT	2♦	1NT	2♥
2♥		2♠	

Hand 1 – 2♦ is a Jacoby Transfer, it is a relay to 2♥. Opener **must** bid hearts.

Hand 2 – 2♥ is a Jacoby Transfer, it is a relay to 2♠. Opener **must** bid spades.

A Jacoby Transfer does not ask opener if he has three or more spades or three or more hearts. It does not ask opener if he has a long suit. It does not ask opener the strength of his NT. It does not ask if opener wants to play in two of a major – it simply **requires** opener to make the forced bid.

Jacoby Transfers is used:

- After a 1NT opening bid or overcall;
- After a 2NT opening bid or two-level or three-level, non-jump overcall of NT;
- After a Strong 2♣ opener and a NT rebid (which you will learn in later classes);
- After an opponent's double of opener's NT bid (which you will learn in later classes); and
- After an opponent's overcall of 2♣, when 2♣ was a conventional (artificial) bid (which you will learn in later classes).

Jacoby Transfers cannot be used:

- After a 1NT or 2NT rebid by opener;
- After a suit overcall by an opponent (other than the artificial 2♣ bid referenced above.

Responders' second bid will show the strength of his hand, the length of his suit and sometimes the distribution of the remainder of his hand. After partner opens or overcalls NT and responder transfers, the bids are simple.

North   South

1NT   2♦

 2♥   ?

South's second bid tells North more about his hand. With:

0-7 HCPs

- Pass

8-9 HCPs

- With only five hearts bid 2NT, and
- With six or more hearts bid 3♥.

10-14 HCPs

- With only five hearts bid 3NT, and
- With six or more hearts bid 4♥.

- A new suit at the three-level is a natural, five-card or longer suit, forcing to game and indicating the possibility of slam.

Transferring to spades works the same way. The auction starts:

North	South
1NT	2♥
2♠	?

South's second bid tells North more about his hand. With:

0-7 HCPs

- Pass

8-9 HCPs

- With only five spades bid 2NT, and
- With six or more spades bid 3♠.

10-14 HCPs

- With only five spades bid 3NT, and
- With six or more spades bid 4♠.

- A new suit at the three-level is a natural, five-card or longer suit, forcing to game and indicating the possibility of slam.

Opener's third bid will be based on:

- The information received from responder's second bid;
- The strength of opener's hand; and
- The number of cards opener holds in responder's major.

Responder Rebid Pass

When responder's second bid was pass (showing 0-7 points), Opener is not going to get another chance to bid so the auction is over and your partnership will play responder's major suit at the two-level.

Responder Rebid 2NT

When responder's second bid was 2NT (showing only five cards in his major suit and 8-9 points) and opener has:

Two cards in responder's major, opener will
- Pass 2NT with 15 HCPs,
- Bid 3NT with 17 HCPs,
- Decide what to do with 16 HCPs based on how valuable opener believes his hand will be in attempting to take nine tricks.

Three or more cards in responder's major, opener will

- Return to responder's major suit at the three-level with 15 points; or
- Return to responder's major at the four-level (game) with 16-17 points.

Responder Rebid 3NT

When responder's second bid was 3NT (showing only five cards in his major suit and 10-14 points) and opener has:

Two cards in responder's major, opener will:
- Pass 3NT, regardless of the strength of his hand.

Three or more cards in responder's major opener will:

- Return to responder's major at the four-level (game).

Responder Rebid his Major at the Three-level (3♥ or 3♠)

When responder's rebid was 3♥/3♠ (showing six cards or more in his major suit and 8-9 points), opener will:

- Pass with 15 points; or
- Bid responder's major at the four-level (game) with 16-17 points.

Responder Rebid his Major at the Four-level (4♥ or 4♠)

When responder's rebid was 4♥/4♠ (showing six cards or more in his major suit and 10-14 points), opener will:

- Pass, **regardless** of the strength of his hand.

Responder Rebid a New Suit at the Three-level

When responder's rebid was a new suit (usually a minor suit) at the three-level (showing a natural, five-card or longer suit, forcing to game and indicating the possibility of slam), opener will:

- Return to responder's major at the three-level with three-card or longer support for the major suit AND a hand that thinks slam is a possibility;
- Bid a new suit, as a cuebid of a control (an Ace) with support for responder's second suit AND a hand that thinks slam is a possibility;
- Return to responder's major suit at the four-level (game) with three-card or longer support for the major AND a hand that thinks slam is unlikely; or
- Bid 3NT with no fit for either of responder's suits AND a hand that thinks slam is unlikely.

Jacoby Transfers

Board 1
North Deals
None Vul

♠ A J 5
♥ K 7
♦ Q 10 9 8
♣ A K 7 4

♠ 3 2
♥ A J 10 4
♦ K J 5 2
♣ 10 5 3

	N	
W		E
	S	

♠ 10 7 6
♥ 9 8 5 2
♦ A 6 4
♣ J 8 2

♠ K Q 9 8 4
♥ Q 6 3
♦ 7 3
♣ Q 9 6

West	North	East	South
	1 N	Pass	2 ♥
Pass	2 ♠	Pass	2 N
Pass	4 ♠	Pass	Pass
Pass			

2♥ = A Jacoby Transfer, forcing partner to bid 2♠.

2NT = I have only five spades and 8-9 points.

4♠ = I have a spade fit (three or more cards) and the values for game (16-17 points).

Jacoby Transfers

Board 2
East Deals
N-S Vul

♠ Q 9 2
♥ A 9 4
♦ K 6 5 2
♣ Q 6 2

♠ 6 3
♥ K J 8 7 5 3
♦ 9 4
♣ 10 8 5

♠ A K 7 4
♥ 6 2
♦ Q J 10 7
♣ A J 7

♠ J 10 8 5
♥ Q 10
♦ A 8 3
♣ K 9 4 3

West	North	East	South
		1 N	Pass
2 ♦	Pass	2 ♥	Pass
Pass	Pass		

2 ♦ = A Jacoby Transfer, forcing partner to bid 2 ♥.

Pass = I have 0-7 points.

Jacoby Transfers

Board 3
South Deals
E-W Vul

♠ A J 8 4 3 2
♥ K 8
♦ K 9 5
♣ 8 3

	N	
♠ 9		♠ 10 5
♥ J 7 5 2	W E	♥ Q 10 6 4
♦ J 10 8 7		♦ 6 4 2
♣ K J 7 5	S	♣ A 10 4 2

♠ K Q 7 6
♥ A 9 3
♦ A Q 3
♣ Q 9 6

West	North	East	South
			1 N
Pass	2 ♥	Pass	2 ♠
Pass	4 ♠	Pass	Pass
Pass			

2♥ = A Jacoby Transfer, forcing partner to bid 2♠.

4♠ = "Partner I have six or more spades and 10-14 points."

Jacoby Transfers

Board 4
West Deals
Both Vul

                    ♠ Q 5 4 2
                    ♥ 6 5 2
                    ♦ K J 3
                    ♣ Q 10 7

♠ K 9 6   ♠ A 3
♥ Q 8   ♥ K J 9 7 3
♦ A Q 10 6      ♦ 9 8 4
♣ K J 8 4   ♣ 9 3 2

                    ♠ J 10 8 7
                    ♥ A 10 4
                    ♦ 7 5 2
                    ♣ A 6 5

West	North	East	South
1 N	Pass	2 ♦	Pass
2 ♥	Pass	2 N	Pass
Pass	Pass		

2 ♦ = A Jacoby Transfer, forcing opener to bid 2 ♥.

2N = "Partner, I have only five hearts and 8-9 points."

Pass = I have only two hearts and only 15-16 points.

Stayman

Stayman is the convention that allows you to discover your four-four card fit after a No Trump opening bid. After an opening bid of 1NT, a bid of 2♣ by responder is Stayman. Responder may not have any clubs, the bid is completely artificial. It simply asks a question - "Partner, do you have a four card major suit?" It promises **at least 8 HCPs and at least one four card major suit**. Responder may also hold a five-card or even six-card major suit.

- Opener has a choice of three bids:
- 2♦ which says, "No, I do not have a four-card, or longer, major suit.";
- 2♥ which says, "Yes, I have four hearts. I may have four spades also."
  (If you have four hearts and four spades, bid hearts); or
- 2♠ which says, "Yes, I have four spades. I do not have four hearts."

Responder's second bid is determined by three factors:
- Whether or not opener bid the major suit in which responder had four-cards or more;

- Whether responder has a five-card major suit as well as a four-card major suit; and
- The strength of responder's hand.

If opener's bid confirmed at least an eight-card suit fit (i.e. showed four cards in a major suit in which responder also had four cards), then responder will raise the major suit to:

- The three level with 8-9 points; or,
- The four level with 10-14 points; or,
- Delay raising the major suit immediately, to make a forcing bid with 15+ points to elicit more information to see if slam is possible.

If opener's bid did not confirm at least an eight-card suit fit (i.e. did not show four cards in a major suit in which responder also had four cards), then responder will:

- Bid 2NT with 8-9 points; or,
- Bid his five-card major suit at the two-level with 8-9 points; or,
- Bid 3NT with 10-14 points; or,
- Bid his five-card major suit at the three-level with 10-14 points,
- Bid a new suit at the three-level.

Stayman

Board 1
North Deals
None Vul

	♠ 10 7 6 2	
	♥ J 7 4	
	♦ A Q 2	
	♣ K J 4	

♠ 8 3   ♠ K Q 9
♥ 5 2   N   ♥ Q 10 6 3
♦ 7 6 5 4 3   W   E   ♦ K J 10
♣ 8 7 6 3   S   ♣ Q 10 9

	♠ A J 5 4	
	♥ A K 9 8	
	♦ 9 8	
	♣ A 5 2	

West	North	East	South
	Pass	1 ♣	1 N
Pass	2 ♣	Pass	2 ♥
Pass	3 N	Pass	4 ♠
Pass	Pass	Pass	

1NT = 15-18 points, a stopper in clubs, and a balanced hand.

2♣ = Stayman asking the NT bidder if he has a four-card major suit.

2♥ = I have four hearts.

3NT = I have the values to bid game and do not have four-card heart support.

4♠ = I have four spades as well as four hearts. **_Remember, North knows that South would not have bid Stayman without at least one four-card major suit. Since South did not have four hearts, South must have four spades._**

Stayman

Board 2

East Deals

N-S Vul

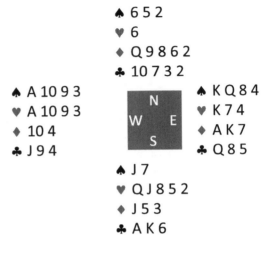

♠ 6 5 2
♥ 6
♦ Q 9 8 6 2
♣ 10 7 3 2

♠ A 10 9 3
♥ A 10 9 3
♦ 10 4
♣ J 9 4

♠ K Q 8 4
♥ K 7 4
♦ A K 7
♣ Q 8 5

♠ J 7
♥ Q J 8 5 2
♦ J 5 3
♣ A K 6

West	North	East	South
		1 N	Pass
2 ♣	Pass	2 ♠	Pass
3 ♠	Pass	4 ♠	Pass
Pass	Pass		

1NT = 15-17 HCPs, a balanced hand and no five-card or longer major suit.

2♣ = Stayman, "Do you have a four card major suit?"

2♠ = I have four spades.

3♠ = I have four spades, we have a fit but I only have 8-9 points.

4♠ = I have a maximum for my NT bid and believe we can make game.

Stayman

Board 3

South Deals

E-W Vul

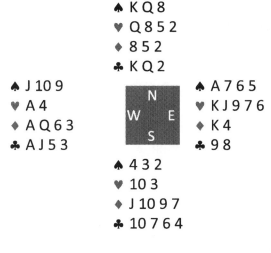

	♠ K Q 8	
	♥ Q 8 5 2	
	♦ 8 5 2	
	♣ K Q 2	

♠ J 10 9 ♠ A 7 6 5
♥ A 4 ♥ K J 9 7 6
♦ A Q 6 3 ♦ K 4
♣ A J 5 3 ♣ 9 8

♠ 4 3 2
♥ 10 3
♦ J 10 9 7
♣ 10 7 6 4

West	North	East	South
			Pass
1 N	Pass	2 ♣	Pass
2 ♦	Pass	3 ♥	Pass
3 N	Pass	Pass	Pass

1NT = 15-17 HCPs, a balanced hand and no five-card or longer major suit.

2♣ = Stayman, asking "Do you have a four-card major suit?"

2♦ = "No, I do not have a four-card major suit."

3♥ = I have five hearts and 10+ points. ***Remember, jumping to the three-level shows the values for game.***

3NT = I don't have a fit (three cards) in hearts.

Stayman

Board 4
West Deals
Both Vul

♠ K 10 6 2
♥ 10 8
♦ A J 8
♣ A K 6 5

♠ Q J 4 3
♥ J 7 4
♦ 9 6 5
♣ 10 9 4

♠ A 8
♥ 9 5 3 2
♦ K Q 7 3
♣ Q J 2

♠ 9 7 5
♥ A K Q 6
♦ 10 4 2
♣ 8 7 3

West	North	East	South
Pass	1 N	Pass	2 ♣
Pass	2 ♠	Pass	2 N
Pass	Pass	Pass	

1NT = 15-17 HCPs, a balanced hand and no five-card or longer major suit.

2 ♣ = Stayman, "Do you have a four card major suit?"

2 ♠ = I have four spades.

2NT = Spades is not the major suit I have. I only have 8-9 points.

Pass = I have a minimum NT hand.

Responding to a 1NT Opening Bid

After your partner has opened 1NT, what would you bid with the following hands?

1) ♠Q2 ♥A7432 ♦A65 ♣73_____

2) ♠7542 ♥A72 ♦65 ♣AJ93_____

3) ♠Q2 ♥872 ♦965 ♣AKJ93_____

4) ♠Q2 ♥AQ72 ♦A65 ♣QJ93_____

5) ♠Q32 ♥J72 ♦65 ♣98543_____

EXTRA CREDIT

If you had the hand below and opened 1NT and your partner bid 2♣ what would you bid as your next bid?

♠Q2 ♥A72 ♦A65 ♣AKT93 _____

Beginner Review

Board 1
North Deals
None Vul

	♠ 10 7 6 2	
	♥ 10 9 7 4	
	♦ A Q	
	♣ Q J 4	

♠ 8 3		♠ K Q 9
♥ 5 2	N	♥ Q J 6 3
♦ K 6 5 4 3	W E	♦ J 10 7
♣ 8 7 6 3	S	♣ 10 9 5

	♠ A J 5 4	
	♥ A K 8	
	♦ 9 8 2	
	♣ A K 2	

West	North	East	South
	Pass	Pass	1 ♣
Pass	1 ♥	Pass	1 ♠
Pass	2 ♠	Pass	4 ♠
Pass	Pass	Pass	

Opening Lead: 4♦ (fourth from your longest and strongest)

1♣ = 3+ clubs and 12+ points.

1♥ = 4+ hearts and 6+ points (6-11 since North passed orignally).

1♠ = I have four spades. I do not have four hearts.

2♠ = I have four spades and 6-9 points.

4♠ = I have enough points for game.

Beginner Review

Board 2
East Deals
N-S Vul

	♠ 6 5 2	
	♥ 8 6	
	♦ K Q 9 6	
	♣ A 7 3 2	

♠ 10 3		♠ K Q J 8 4
♥ A Q J 10 3	N	♥ 7 4 2
♦ J 4 3	W E	♦ A 8 7
♣ K 6 4	S	♣ Q 5

	♠ A 9 7	
	♥ K 9 5	
	♦ 10 5 2	
	♣ J 10 9 8	

West	North	East	South
		1 ♠	Pass
2 ♥	Pass	3 ♥	Pass
Pass	Pass		

Opening Lead: K ♦ (top of touching honors)

1♠ = 5+ spades and 12+ points.

2♥ = 5+ hearts and 10+ points.

3♥ = 12/13 points and 3+ hearts.

Pass = I had only 10/11 points.

Beginner Review

Board 3

South Deals

E-W Vul

```
                        ♠ 8 5
                        ♥ A 8 5
                        ♦ 8 5
                        ♣ A K Q J 3 2
    ♠ Q J 10 9                        ♠ K 7 6
    ♥ Q J 7 4 2          N            ♥ K 9 6
    ♦ Q 10 3          W     E         ♦ A 6 4 2
    ♣ 5                  S            ♣ 10 9 8
                        ♠ A 4 3 2
                        ♥ 10 3
                        ♦ K J 9 7
                        ♣ 7 6 4
```

West	North	East	South
			Pass
Pass	1 ♣	Pass	1 ♠
Pass	2 ♣	Pass	Pass
Pass			

Opening Lead: ♥6 (low from an honor in the unbid suit)

1♣ = 3+ clubs and 12+ points

1♠ = 4+ spades and 6+ points

2♣ = 5+ clubs and 12-14/15 points

Beginner Review

Board 4
West Deals
Both Vul

♠ Q J 10 5 3
♥ J 7 4 2
♦ 10 6
♣ K 4

♠ A 9 7 4
♥ Q 6 5
♦ 9 7 2
♣ 10 6 3

N
W E
S

♠ K 2
♥ A 10 8
♦ A Q 8 5
♣ A J 7 5

♠ 8 6
♥ K 9 3
♦ K J 4 3
♣ Q 9 8 2

West	North	East	South
Pass	Pass	1 ♦	Pass
1 ♠	Pass	2 N	Pass
Pass	Pass		

Opening Lead: 2 ♣

1 ♦ = 3+ diamonds and 12+ points

1 ♠ = 4+ spades and 6+ points

2N = 18-19 points and no spade fit

Pass = I have a really, really bad hand!

Overcall

When a player opens the bidding, up to now, the other partnership has been silent. Not any more!

After an opponent opens the bidding, a player from the other partnership is still allowed to bid. If they choose to bid, that bid is called an '***overcall***'. The player making the bid is called the '***Overcaller***' and his partner is called '***Advancer***'. Unlike an opening bid an overcall is a limited to bid showing 8-17 HCPs.

A typical overcall promises:

- 5+ cards in the suit he bids, and
- 2 top honors (Ace, King, Queen or Jack), and
- About 10 HCPs.

When overcaller has a really strong hand, he could overcall with a suit that isn't as strong as we expect.

When overcaller has a really strong suit (three honors or extra length), he could choose to bid with less than 10 HCPs.

However, an overcall must always show a five-card or longer suit!

Responding to an Overcall

In responding to an overcall, the requirements are about the same as when partner has opened the bidding, just remember that partner only has to have 10 points to overcall.

Advancer's Bid

If you don't have a fit for overcaller's suit you should say to yourself "I think I should pass".

Your partner is unlikely to have a match for your suit since we know he has a least five-cards in his own suit. Overcaller might also have a weakish hand.

You should only bid a new suit if you have:

- A pretty good hand yourself (about 9 HCPs or so) and at least five cards in your suit, or
- A really long suit (7 cards or so) that you plan to bid again.

If you have a fit for overcaller's suit you should say to yourself "I think I should bid".

Later in your bridge studies you'll learn some special bids that you can use to raise partner's overcall. For right now just pretend that partner opened showing a five-card or longer suit (remembering that overcaller might have a weaker hand).

With at least three-card support for Overcaller's suit:

With 6 to 9 or 10 HCPs – Raise one-level.

With 10 to 12 or 13 HCPs – Raise two-levels.

With 13 or more HCPs – Raise a major suit to game. If partner overcalled a minor suit, see if it's possible to play in a No Trump game.

Remember when overcalling

The longer and better your suit, the less high card points you must have.

The worse and shorter your suit, the more high card points or better distribution you must have.

DEFINITIONS

Bid - A call by which a player shares information about his hand with his partner and eventually proposes a contract that his side will win at least as many tricks as his bid specifies

Bidding - The period following the deal, and ending after the third successive pass of any bid

Book - The first six tricks won by a declarer contract - The undertaking by declarer's side to win, at the denomination named, the number of tricks specified in the final bid

Contract - The undertaking by declarer's side to win, at the denomination named, the number of tricks specified in the final bid

Declarer - The player who first bid the suit (or no trump) which became the final bid.

Distribution - The manner in which the cards of a suit are dispersed among the four hands of a deal, or the manner in which the number of cards in the four suits are distributed in one hand

Dummy - The declarer's partner after he has placed his cards face up on the table immediately after the opponent to declarer's left has made their opening lead

Final Bid - The last bid in the auction, followed by three consecutive passes. The final bid becomes the contract

Finesse - The attempt to gain power for lower-ranking cards by taking advantage of the favorable position of higher ranking cards

Game Contract - An undertaking of a contract which, if successful, will earn enough points to make the 100 points necessary for a game and award a 300 to 500 point bonus

Lead - The first card played to a trick

Opening Lead - The first card played by the person to declarer's left

Opponent - A member of the adverse team at bridge

Partner - The player with whom one is paired in a game of bridge

Trick - Consists of four cards played in rotation after an initial lead of one of the cards by the player whose turn it was to lead

Trick-Score - The value of each trick of fulfilled contracts towards the winning of the game

Trump - The suit named in the final bid, other than No Trump. Such suit is called the 'trump suit' and a card of the trump suit, when played, is a winner over any card of another suit

Vulnerable - a term indicating that the values of premiums and the severity of penalties are greatly increased

Quiz - The Basics

1) How many cards are there in a deck of cards? __52__

2) What are the four suits? __spades_____   -
   ____hearts__ _diamonds_   ___clubs_

3) How many tricks are there in every hand you play?
   _13_

4) What is the highest card in the deck?___Ace____

5) **Who wins the trick in a No Trump hand? The player
   who plays the highest card in the suit led.**

   _____

EXTRA CREDIT

Explain trumps. ___a suit maybe declared trumps in
the bidding. If you have a trump suit then the
highest trump played on a trick wins, no matter how
small it is._____

Bridge with Patty!

Quiz - Scoring

1) Which are the major suits? __spades_
   __hearts___
2) Which are the minor suits? __diamonds__   -
   __clubs__
3) How many points do you get for every trick in a
   minor suit? __20___
4) If you bid 4♣, how many tricks would you need
   to win to make your contract ? __10, book plus
   the number I bid____
5) What is book? ___the first six tricks won by
   the declaring side_____

EXTRA CREDIT

If your contract is 3♠ and you win ten tricks, how
many points would you earn?   **170**

Ten – book (6) = 4

4 x 30 points for each trick = 120

Bonus for a part-score = 50

120+50 = 170

Quiz - Bidding

1) How many points can you count for each of the honor cards?
Ace _**4**__ King_**3**_Queen_**2**__Jack_**1**_Ten__**0**____

2) Which player has the first chance to open the bidding?
__**the person who dealt the cards**__

3) How many points do you need to open the bidding?__**12**__

4) What is the first thing you look for when you are deciding what to open? __**do I have a five-card or longer major (hearts or spades)**__

5) How many cards do you need in a minor suit to open the bidding 1♣ or 1♦?
_____**three**_____

EXTRA CREDIT

If you do not have five cards or more in a major suit and you hold three clubs and three diamonds, which suit would you open? ____**clubs - I would bid 1♣**__

Responding to the Opening Bid

1) When your partner opens the bidding, what person do you become?_**Responder**_

2) How many points do you need to respond to the opening bidder? ___**6**___

3) When your partner opens a minor suit and you have enough points to respond, what is the first thing you look for in your hand?_**do I have four or more cards in either hearts or spades (a major suit)**_

4) After partner has opened 1♣, how many cards do you need in hearts in order to bid 1♥? ___**at least four**___

5) After partner has opened 1♠, how many high card points (HCPs) and how many cards do you need in hearts in order to bid 2♥?

   # of Hearts needed __**5**_ HCPs needed_**at least 10**___

EXTRA CREDIT

In the bidding, what is ranking of the four suits and No Trump?

_clubs__ _diamonds__ hearts_ __spades_ _NoTrump_

Lowest   Highest

Quiz - Opener and Responder Rebids

1) Every time you bid what are you describing about your hand?__Strength__ and __distribution___

2) When you open 1♣ and responder bids 1♥, how many hearts do you need to raise responder's heart suit? __four because responder promised four and we are looking for eight between our two hands__

3) When opener raises responder's heart suit to 3♥, how many points does opener promise?_a medium hand. 16-18 points or a really good 15 point hand._

4) When responder raises opener's 1♠ opening bid to 2♠ and opener holds 19 HCPs, what should opener's bid as his second bid? _4♠_Opener knows they have at least 25 points which should be enough to bid game.

5) After opener has opened 1♠ and responder has bid 1NT, how many points and how many spades would opener promise if he bid 3♠?

   # of Spades needed ___6___ HCPs needed__16__

EXTRA CREDIT

If you had the hand below and opened 1♣ and your partner bid 1♠, what would you bid as your second bid?

♠Q2 ♥A72 ♦A65 ♣AKJ93

2NT

Responding to a 1NT Opening Bid

After your partner has opened 1NT, what would you bid with the following hands?

6) ♠Q2 ♥A7432 ♦A65 ♣73____**a Jacoby Transfer, 2♦_**

7) ♠7542 ♥A72 ♦65 ♣AJ93___**Stayman, 2♣____**

8) ♠Q2 ♥872 ♦965 ♣AKJ93__**3NT___**

9) ♠Q2 ♥AQ72 ♦A65 ♣QJ93_ **Stayman, 2♣____**

10) ♠Q32 ♥J72 ♦65 ♣98543__**Pass____**

EXTRA CREDIT

If you had the hand below and opened 1NT and your partner bid 2♣ what would you bid as your next bid?

♠Q2 ♥A72 ♦A65 ♣AKT93 _**2♦_Telling partner that I did not have a four-card major suit.__**

About the Author

Patty Tucker

Patty learned to play bridge in 1964 at the age of eleven and became a full-time bridge teacher in 1999. A familiar face at regional and national tournaments, Patty received national recognition upon winning the 2000 North American Open Pairs National Championship with long-time partner and husband, Kevin Collins. From Patty, "I teach for the immense satisfaction I get in passing on to others my love for the game of bridge".

Major Accomplishments:

- Georgia Bridge Hall of Fame (2012)
- ACBL Goodwill Member of the Year (2011)
- North American Open Pairs Champion (2000)
- National Goodwill Committee (ACBL)
- Sportsman of the Year, Unit 114 (2000)
- Emerald Life Master
- District 7 Goodwill Member
- National Goodwill Committee (ACBL)
- Unit 114 Recorder
- ACBL Certified Director
- ACBL Accredited Teacher
- American Bridge Teachers Association Master Teacher
- Better Bridge Accredited Teacher
- Co-Founder Whirlwind Bridge
- ACBL Youth Coordinator (May 2008 through December 2009)
- Trustee, Foundation for the Preservation and Advancement of Bridge (FPAB)
- ACBL National Charity Committee

Made in the USA
Middletown, DE
21 August 2016